The Storms Of April & The Ghosts That Whisper My Name

Life Through These Blue Eyes

Rebekah Thomas Logie

BookLeaf Publishing
India | USA | UK

Made with ❤ on the BookLeaf Publishing Platform
www.bookleafpub.in
www.bookleafpub.com

Dedication

Unbreakable. Resilient. Survivor.
Miss Independent -
but the walls of my fortress were built on sinking ground.
Never asking for help, never reaching for a hand.

I put myself here, but who can I trust?
Give your love. Give your soul. Give your life.
Gave it all for a lover who favored lust.

The trauma of trying, of caring too much.
I sought freedom from another
but he decided my life wasn't worth enough.

"Friends" turned away when my days turned dark,
praised me to my face, then slandered my name.
Alcohol and drugs to numb the pain,
while my favorite songs don't sound the same.

I do it all solo,
always alone to pick up the pieces. Reparo.
But I'm too broken.
No longer resilient.
No longer sure I want to survive.

The darkness is winning... I think it's time...

Then I see you.

Big brown eyes, wide with wonder.
Perfect curls, a smile I grew within me.
The sweetest voice calling- Mama.

So tonight,
I'll stay a little longer in the shower,
silently scream, try to take back my power.
I'll call my therapist, book extra hours.

And I'll push forward, like I always do.
For you. Only for you.

...Thank you.

Preface

When I look back on my life,
I often wonder how many people have I truly impacted?
Have I even made a difference,
outside of my own flesh and blood,
the ones bound to me by obligation?

Will the others remember me
once the funeral is over,
once their heartfelt posts
drift down their feeds,
once life resumes its usual rhythm?
Will they still care
when the attention is no longer on them?

How will they remember me?
As anxious yet kind,
caring yet wild,
flirtatious and fun,
sassy and independent,
tenacious and empathetic?

Or simply as the redhead with blue eyes,
the one who cursed too much,
let emotions rule her,

was always down for a shot -
but Irish-goodbyed after too many?

The one who spoke passionately
but only about a few things?
I can only hope I've left
a trace of kindness in my wake.

Because in the end,
it's not about career milestones
or net worth,
not about weight
or physical beauty.

It's about how you make people feel.
That's your legacy.

So be kind, always.
Speak life into others.
Put ego aside.
Listen - truly listen.
Hug them often.
Support their dreams.
Hold their hand through the storms.

Life is so short.

Embrace it.
Embrace them.

Acknowledgements

These are my vulnerable thoughts captured poetically. I hope they make you feel something. Enjoy!

1. Siren's Rage, Mermaid's Grace

A tidebound choice-
standing at the water's edge,
torn between becoming
a mermaid who sings to soothe the sea
or a siren who sings ships to their doom.

What does it feel like
to trade your legs for a tail?
To swim the line
between allure and grace?

The siren's regret,
the mermaid's longing-
two sides of the same salt-soaked coin.

I hear the call of the deep:
two songs rise from the ocean,
one haunting, one healing.

My scales shimmer like secrets.
My voice-
a gift for the abyss,
holds the power

either to lure or to love.

Pearls or storms-
one life offers soft coral beds
and gentle companionship;
the other,
lightning in my throat
and tempests under my skin.

Where do I belong?

Human no more-
should I slip into the siren's rage,
or the mermaid's serenity?

2. The Cactus On the Windowsill Whispers Secrets to the Moon When No One's Looking

I built this fortress with shaking hands,
Lived through the struggle of constructing strength,
while secretly wishing someone would notice the cracks

Don't rescue me,
I am not a damsel in destress,
Just sit beside me while I figure it out
Companionship without dependency,

There's pride in my silence,
and pain too
The price of self-reliance when vulnerability feels too risky,
Is everything

Teach me how to need without guilt,
Help me unlearn the shame that lives with in
I can carry it, I always have,
But maybe I don't want to anymore?

I keep my hands in my pockets,
Not because I don't want to hold yours,
But because I'm scared I'll never let go

I am both the storm,
and the one seeking shelter
strong and vulnerable,
Self-sufficient and also in need.

I said 'I'm fine' with a voice that hoped you'd stay
anyway.

3. Fragments of My Forgotten Soul

I look into my shattered mirror,
my reflection breaking into a thousand selves,
each one vying for dominance
I gather the shards, piece by piece,
trying to rebuild a mosaic of me,
yet the final picture is a stranger's face

A name written in water,
I try to carve letters into the river's flow,
grasp at steam, only to watch it slip away
What happens when even your own essence dissolves
within your very hands?

My body has become an uncharted map,
its terrain claimed by foreign cartographers,
What landmarks remain mine?
Which shall I erase?

I stand as a house of cards,
each one representing who I thought I was,
teetering at the mercy of the slightest breeze
I prepare for collapse,
there is no strong foundation here

A chameleon without control,
I bleed into every background,
forgetting the hue that once was mine
How do I mourn the loss of my own vibrancy?

I salvage scraps of my story,
a burning manuscript with pages scorched
I let the ashes settle in my lungs,
the breath of failed rewrites choking me

I am a torn painting,
a masterpiece defaced by time
vandalized by misfortunate touches,
I long for the brushstrokes that once defined me

And so I drift,
an orphaned shadow,
aimless, figureless,
reaching for something solid,
a wall, a hand, your chest, a place to rest

As I look through my collection of borrowed masks,
faces stitched together from others' truths
None fit anymore,
I stumble around in panic,
forgetting the face I once called my own

4. I Broke My Favorite Mug This AM

I am a porcelain mug, delicate
But with the weight of stone
Still, even stone can crumble

High on the top shelf
Hanging on the very edge
One more slammed door
Or raised voice near me
Will cause me to quiver
And fall

The floor waiting
As I am suspended in stillness
Then in a heartbeat

Shattered

Into fragments of a story never told
A history of whispered wounds
Broken beyond repair
Echoing with the jagged sound of broken glass
Shards sparkle like forgotten stars
A thousand echoes of silence

As the world forgets
That I was ever whole

5. You're Not Ugly, You're Just Poor

As I stare into the mirror,
wrinkles crease my forehead,
stretch marks reach across my hips,
my thighs touch as I walk.

Cellulite, extra fat, unwanted hairs—
I could stand here for hours,
staring at my flaws,
tearing myself down.

I don't look like the women on IG,
or the ones on TV,
or the perfectly sculpted figures in magazines.

I grew up in the Kate Moss cocaine era,
thin like Paris Hilton and Lindsay Lohan.
"America's Next Top Model"—"You're too fat."
Rib cages, hip bones, the lowest-rise jeans.
A size 6 was seen as obese.

Jessica Simpson in high-waisted jeans,
a size 10, unworthy of Abercrombie.
So I punished myself for having curves—

200 crunches for 200 calories,
work out to eat, starve to feel pretty.

Until fatigue and hunger set in.
Binge on everything in sight.
Then the guilt.
Wake up, repeat.

But society has shifted from my days of super thin—
BBLs, comically huge lips, plastic cheeks,
fillers and watermelon-sized tits.
Layers of contoured makeup
to hide a single blemish.

Filters and FaceTune—who even are you?
They scream inclusivity, but only if you look like them.
Mormon stay-at-home wives with Botox highs.
To each their own,
self-love for the win.

But when will natural beauty actually be in?
And how do we teach our little girls
to love themselves from within
when every screen tells them-
You're not enough.
You need to look like this to fit in.
Flawless white teeth, perfect skin.

Maybe it's time to redefine beauty-
to see past the filters and facades,
to and value in scars and imperfections.

Or maybe the world will never let us be
free from its ideals of feminine beauty.

All I know is-
this endless search is exhausting,
and I'm still trying to love what I see.

6. I Have No Concept of Time, Yet it Controls Me

Tick, tock, tick, tock-
I watch the hands of the clock,
chasing my every thought.

So much to do, no time to stop-
rush here, rush there,
always fucking late.

No space to breathe,
I'm chasing fate,
never enough time,
too much on my plate.

Tick, tock, tick, tock-
one day, I'll smash that
controlling little clock

7. Choose Your Garden Carefully

There she stood, the most coveted treasure-
a bloom of rare beauty,
her petals vibrant with color,
her scent a dance of honeydew and gypsy rain.

And she was his, finally.

After years of searching, of aching want,
he held his most precious flower.
The envy of all, his friends gawked at her grace,
and their words filled him with pride.
Oh, how he loved his newfound prize.

He adorned her with praises often,
pruned her tenderly—no leaf left to brown.
In her presence, he felt alive with purpose,
daydreaming of her even when apart.
Radiant and cherished, he cared only about her.

But one day, he grew weary.

His hands, once gentle,
grew heavy with neglect.

And his words, once filled with love,
turned sharp and sparse.

Her care became a burden too great,
her blooms a responsibility he no longer craved.
Day by day, his eyes forgot to linger.

Her petals, once his pride, began to wilt,
leaves curling into signs of abandonment.
"I'll tend to her tomorrow," he'd say,
but tomorrow never came.

And so, she faded.

Once a gorgeous symphony of life,
now only brittle stems and decaying roots remained-
a hushed echo of what once was.

8. Gas Station Bathrooms with the Key Zip Tied to a Hole in a Plunger Rod

Flip the light switch on
Watch the walls become alive
Roaches scatter, vanishing into cracks
too small to even exist
but they do

The lights flicker above
a dull hum fills the room
air thick with feces and neglect
The sour scent clings to me unshakable,
a vile second skin

I shake my head
choking on the bile of regret
asking myself again
how did I end up here?
Every decision feels so distant
blurred by time or perhaps,
desperate denial

Do I risk the disease

the crawl of infection hiding
beneath every surface?
Would anyone else walk away?
Would they burn it all down
and start over?
What's a girl supposed to do?

9. Ten Deadly Sins, and I am One of Them

She is wild like thunder,
yet sweet like rain.
She cries into the sunflowers,
her love a hunger pang.

She carries a sunburnt dream
of sweet self-destruction,
painting her petals
in crimson seduction.

She yearns for an Elysian existence,
a lover devoted-
lingering limerence
in every word she wrote.

10. Hey Dreamer

What could you possibly daydream about all day long?

Well, let's see...

What's it like to fly on the back of a dragon?
Imagine traveling the Oregon Trail by wagon.
What if I had a superpower-
which one would I choose?
And what would our feet look like
if we never wore shoes?

I reminisce on that meal in that country,
the one I'd eat every day for a week.
What if dinosaurs didn't roar-
but only squeaked?

What would it be like to grow up in Spain?
How cool would it be to see multicolored rain?
How did this very spot look
100, 100,000, or a million years ago?
And how many kids would pick Raphael
over Michelangelo?

What must it feel like to fear great heights?

How hard was it to battle in a knight's heavy armor?
If I were stranded on an island alone,
would I actually go crazy?
What's a day in the life of Jay-Z?

How would it feel to just disappear?
Would I really trade places with someone else?
The first people to create a language—
how did that even go?
And what if we only saw in shades of red and yellow?

How badly did pirates smell after months at sea?
If I could talk to animals,
what would they say to me?
What does it feel like to be truly seen?
How many alien species exist—
and are any of them green?

What is it like to breathe with gills?
Why do certain things give us chills?
Am I swimming over a dead body?
Who decided "hottie" was a compliment?
And why?

What if I'm actually in a coma,
and this has all been a dream?
What if every day were Halloween?

These are just a few of the thoughts
that float around in my mind—
because daydreaming might just be
the most beautiful way to waste time.

11. Social Chameleon

The intensity and curiosity within me
often make me awkward, force me to screen.
I'll drop a bomb of a thought—
like what flavor is the color green?
Or what if spiders loudly screamed?

Then I cringe, bracing for a scene.
Only a few match my weird energy-
I love them most, keep them close.
But the rest make me put my mask back on,
fear creeping in, rejection looming.

My sensitivity disorder takes over.

"Act normal. Fit into square society."
Okay, let's talk celebrities, TV, trends.
My job keeps me savvy on the mundane,
but it all feels dull, unfulfilling.

And yet... to fit in, that's the game.
(Do I even care, though?)

It's exhausting, shifting my colors so often—
a little social chameleon.

12. You Burn Me Like the Sun, But Your Light is All I Can See

The stars whisper love songs,
so melodies meant only for the moon,
but she turns away, her gaze lost on the horizon,
dreaming of a warmth she can never touch.

An endless cycle—
basking in the sun's glow by day,
left in the cold embrace of the stars by night.
At dawn and dusk,
the moon and sun brush against the edge of eternity,
only to part over and over, forever.

The stars watch, helpless,
as the moon's heart soars for a love
that lasts only seconds.

They give her their brightest light,
hoping to be seen,
but she only reflects the sun.

A celestial heartbreak.

13. Watching the Wind Whisper Through the Trees, Carrying a Thousand Untold Stories

A golden hour revival
the dancing rays of sunlight –
a fresh start,
washing away past sorrows.

Like stepping outside after the storm,
when the rain has stopped,
the world smells new,
and hope lingers in the air.

Windows open, curtains flirting with the wind,
a day so light, so breezy,
even the house breathes easier.

Laughter drifts through the air,
filling the space like music,
making everything feel weightless.

The scent of summer teases,

salt air, fresh-cut grass,
citrus in the breeze.

Today, I fly high, untethered,
catching every gust of wind,
joy soaring like a kite.

14. The Corner of Spiritualist Street and Mediumship Way

Went to Cassadaga to commune with the dead,
how I love this small, quaint town.
Cats wander freely, guardians of the quiet,
a fairy trail calls with whispered magic.

Stand by the lake, let the vortex pull you in,
its unseen force a gentle embrace.
Head to the cemetery, but steer clear
of the Devil's Chair and its chilling lore.

One day, perhaps,
an adorable purple house on the hill
will call me home,
a place of peace amidst the spirits.

15. A Broken Frame (Of Mind)

How dreadful it is
to carry all of this inside me,
but to the others,
they are just words—
scribbles on a page,
emphasized sounds.

How ironic that these words
contain everything inside me.
I could scream at them,
right in their faces,
and they wouldn't feel a thing.

What a burden of emotional turmoil,
what a punishment of depth.
How unfair and cruel—
I am nothing but unhung art,
collecting dust in an attic.

16. Bitch, I'm the Bomb, Like Tick Tick

You throw fuel on my fire
expecting me not be engulfed in flames
And the salt you rub so intently into my wounds
was derived from the tears
streaming down my face

And I am not fragile like porcelain, no,
I am fragile like a bomb,
a wired tight, delicate design,
a gentle balance of tension and intent

And in these most tender moments,
I am forced to decide my fate
for my heart's sake

Do I defuse,
disengage
or duck the fuck outta dodge?

17. The Quiet Art of Falling to Pieces on Paper

Some call it poetry...
I call it carving open my chest,
letting my heart bleed freely.

It's the sound of ribs cracking,
making room for pain to breathe,
tears pressed into paper—
immortal echoes of my trials.

It's the art of caging my emotions,
so I can wear normalcy like armor
for the world outside.

18. Some Books and A Dream

A tiny bookstore on a cobblestone street,
where coffee is poured with the morning light
and cocktails flow as evening settles in.

Local art lines the walls, waiting for a home,
while melodies of nearby musicians drift through the air.
Shelves brim with every genre, always something new to find,
and the scent of old leather and fresh-brewed coffee lingers.

A friendly shop dog greets each visitor,
tail wagging, nose nudging against well-worn pages.
Here, I'd watch my son fall in love with stories,
lose himself in the magic of words.

A place to call my own,
my little bibliophilic dream—
a tiny bookstore on a street of cobblestone.

19. Dodging Waves and Jellyfish, Yet Somehow I Still Find Myself Getting Stung

I watch the jellyfish,
stranded, helpless,
its glass body half-buried in sand,
tentacles reaching, recoiling
as the tide teases, then retreats-
a cruel, indifferent lover.

For a moment, I sit in quiet awe,
until grief swells within me,
rushing in like the tide.

How tragic, how familiar -
to be cast aside,
left out to dry on the shore
by the very thing you loved most.

20. Lessons From the Leaves

I've learned that some seasons bring bloom,
and others,
a quiet dying-
hibernation in waiting.

I've learned to seek the sun,
to turn my face toward
warmth.
Some grow tall, reaching,
while others stretch wide, embracing.

I've learned it's okay to shed leaves
that no longer serve me,
that strong roots matter more
than fleeting blossoms.

I've learned that environment
will shape what thrives,
that the wrong place can wither
even the strongest stem,
and the right one can turn the smallest seed into a forest.

I used to drown my plants in love,
never knowing when

to stop pouring-

sometimes,
I still do.

www.ingramcontent.com/pod-product-compliance
Lightning Source LLC
Chambersburg PA
CBHW051746130826
49812CB00033B/1029
9789370926684